AF380066

Baby Shower For

Date

Guest Name

Relationship to Parents

Advice for Parents

Wishes for Baby

Guest Name

Relationship to Parents

Advice for Parents

Wishes for Baby

Guest Name

Relationship to Parents

Advice for Parents

Wishes for Baby

Guest Name

Relationship to Parents

Advice for Parents

Wishes for Baby

Guest Name

Relationship to Parents

Advice for Parents

Wishes for Baby

Guest Name

Relationship to Parents

Advice for Parents

Wishes for Baby

Guest Name

Relationship to Parents

Advice for Parents

Wishes for Baby

Guest Name

Relationship to Parents

Advice for Parents

Wishes for Baby

Guest Name

Relationship to Parents

Advice for Parents

Wishes for Baby

Guest Name

Relationship to Parents

Advice for Parents

Wishes for Baby

Guest Name

Relationship to Parents

Advice for Parents

Wishes for Baby

Guest Name

Relationship to Parents

Advice for Parents

Wishes for Baby

Guest Name

Relationship to Parents

Advice for Parents

Wishes for Baby

Guest Name

Relationship to Parents

Advice for Parents

Wishes for Baby

Guest Name

Relationship to Parents

Advice for Parents

Wishes for Baby

Guest Name

Relationship to Parents

Advice for Parents

Wishes for Baby

Guest Name

Relationship to Parents

Advice for Parents

Wishes for Baby

Guest Name

Relationship to Parents

Advice for Parents

Wishes for Baby

Guest Name

Relationship to Parents

Advice for Parents

Wishes for Baby

Guest Name

Relationship to Parents

Advice for Parents

Wishes for Baby

Guest Name

Relationship to Parents

Advice for Parents

Wishes for Baby

Guest Name

____

Relationship to Parents

____

Advice for Parents

____

____

____

Wishes for Baby

____

____

____

Guest Name

Relationship to Parents

Advice for Parents

Wishes for Baby

Guest Name

____

Relationship to Parents

____

Advice for Parents

____

____

____

____

Wishes for Baby

____

____

____

Guest Name

Relationship to Parents

Advice for Parents

Wishes for Baby

Guest Name

Relationship to Parents

Advice for Parents

Wishes for Baby

Guest Name

Relationship to Parents

Advice for Parents

Wishes for Baby

Guest Name

Relationship to Parents

Advice for Parents

Wishes for Baby

Guest Name

Relationship to Parents

Advice for Parents

Wishes for Baby

Guest Name

Relationship to Parents

Advice for Parents

Wishes for Baby

Guest Name

Relationship to Parents

Advice for Parents

Wishes for Baby

Guest Name

Relationship to Parents

Advice for Parents

Wishes for Baby

Guest Name

Relationship to Parents

Advice for Parents

Wishes for Baby

Guest Name

Relationship to Parents

Advice for Parents

Wishes for Baby

Guest Name

Relationship to Parents

Advice for Parents

Wishes for Baby

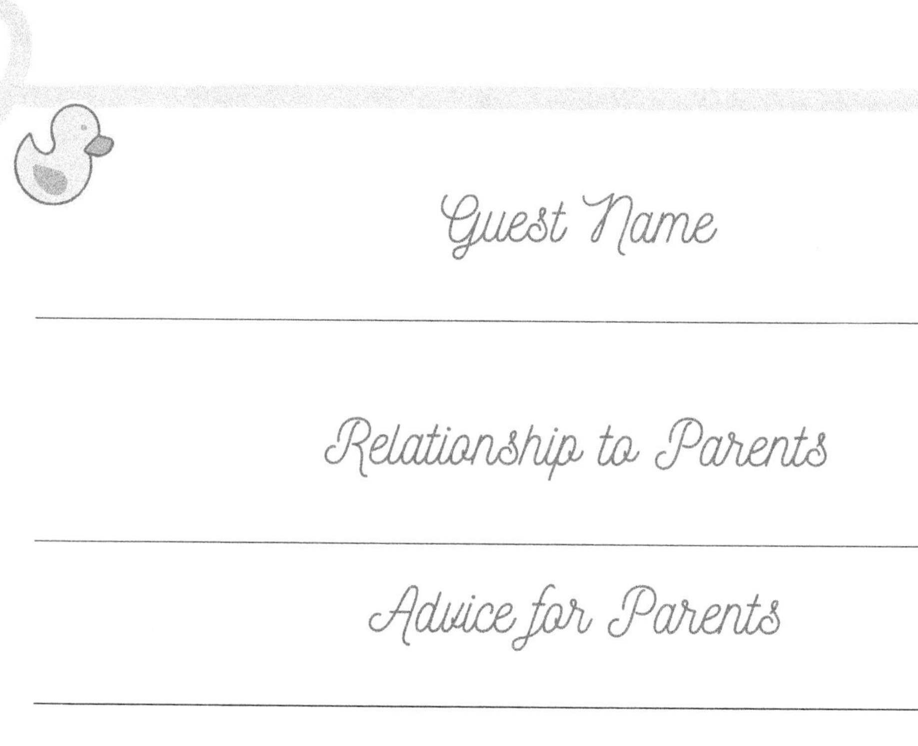

Guest Name

Relationship to Parents

Advice for Parents

Wishes for Baby

Guest Name

Relationship to Parents

Advice for Parents

Wishes for Baby

Guest Name

____

Relationship to Parents

____

Advice for Parents

____

____

____

____

Wishes for Baby

____

____

____

____

Guest Name

Relationship to Parents

Advice for Parents

Wishes for Baby

Guest Name

Relationship to Parents

Advice for Parents

Wishes for Baby

Guest Name

Relationship to Parents

Advice for Parents

Wishes for Baby

Guest Name

Relationship to Parents

Advice for Parents

Wishes for Baby

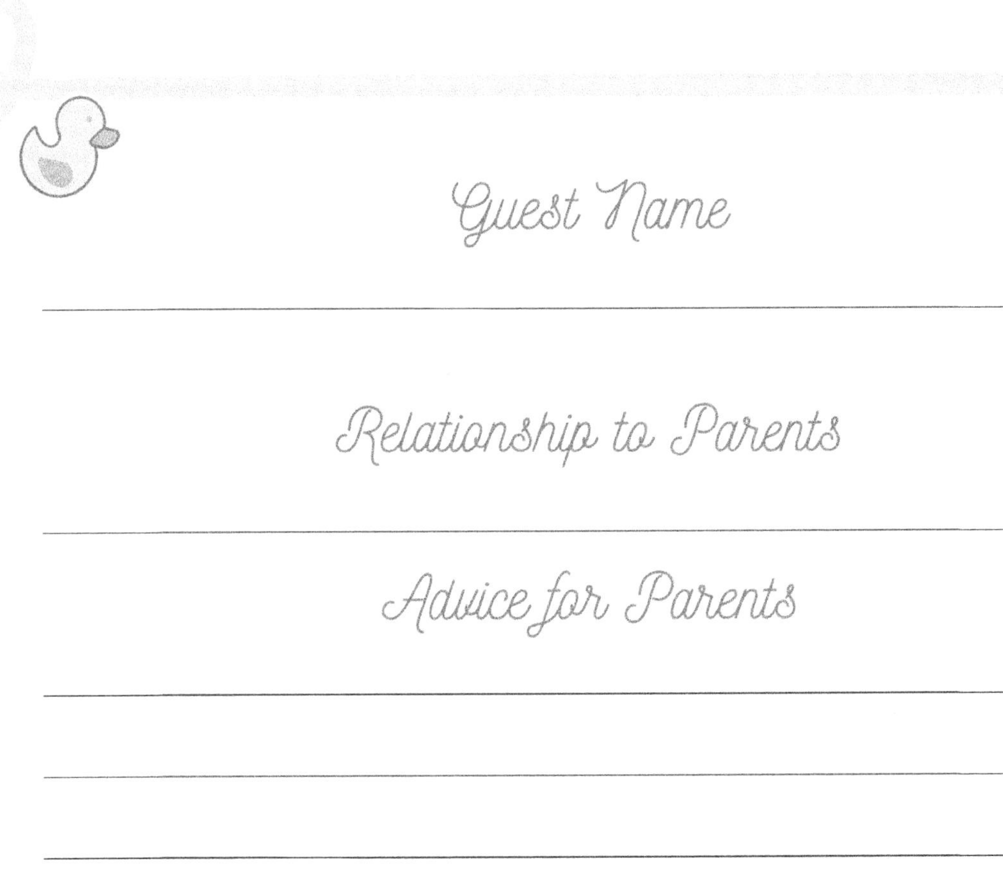

Guest Name

Relationship to Parents

Advice for Parents

Wishes for Baby

Guest Name

Relationship to Parents

Advice for Parents

Wishes for Baby

Guest Name

Relationship to Parents

Advice for Parents

Wishes for Baby

Guest Name

Relationship to Parents

Advice for Parents

Wishes for Baby

Guest Name

____

Relationship to Parents

____

Advice for Parents

____

____

____

____

Wishes for Baby

____

____

____

Guest Name

Relationship to Parents

Advice for Parents

Wishes for Baby

Guest Name

Relationship to Parents

Advice for Parents

Wishes for Baby

Guest Name

Relationship to Parents

Advice for Parents

Wishes for Baby

Guest Name

Relationship to Parents

Advice for Parents

Wishes for Baby

Guest Name

Relationship to Parents

Advice for Parents

Wishes for Baby

Guest Name

Relationship to Parents

Advice for Parents

Wishes for Baby

Guest Name

Relationship to Parents

Advice for Parents

Wishes for Baby

Guest Name

Relationship to Parents

Advice for Parents

Wishes for Baby

Guest Name

Relationship to Parents

Advice for Parents

Wishes for Baby

Guest Name

Relationship to Parents

Advice for Parents

Wishes for Baby

Guest Name

____

Relationship to Parents

____

Advice for Parents

____

____

____

Wishes for Baby

____

____

____

Guest Name

Relationship to Parents

Advice for Parents

Wishes for Baby

Guest Name

Relationship to Parents

Advice for Parents

Wishes for Baby

Guest Name

Relationship to Parents

Advice for Parents

Wishes for Baby

Guest Name

Relationship to Parents

Advice for Parents

Wishes for Baby

Guest Name

Relationship to Parents

Advice for Parents

Wishes for Baby

Guest Name

Relationship to Parents

Advice for Parents

Wishes for Baby

Guest Name

Relationship to Parents

Advice for Parents

Wishes for Baby

Guest Name

____

Relationship to Parents

____

Advice for Parents

____

____

____

____

Wishes for Baby

____

____

____

Guest Name

Relationship to Parents

Advice for Parents

Wishes for Baby

Guest Name

Relationship to Parents

Advice for Parents

Wishes for Baby

Guest Name

Relationship to Parents

Advice for Parents

Wishes for Baby

Guest Name

Relationship to Parents

Advice for Parents

Wishes for Baby

Guest Name

Relationship to Parents

Advice for Parents

Wishes for Baby

Guest Name

Relationship to Parents

Advice for Parents

Wishes for Baby

Guest Name

Relationship to Parents

Advice for Parents

Wishes for Baby

Guest Name

Relationship to Parents

Advice for Parents

Wishes for Baby

Guest Name

Relationship to Parents

Advice for Parents

Wishes for Baby

Guest Name

Relationship to Parents

Advice for Parents

Wishes for Baby

Guest Name

Relationship to Parents

Advice for Parents

Wishes for Baby

Guest Name

Relationship to Parents

Advice for Parents

Wishes for Baby

Guest Name

Relationship to Parents

Advice for Parents

Wishes for Baby

Guest Name

Relationship to Parents

Advice for Parents

Wishes for Baby

Guest Name

Relationship to Parents

Advice for Parents

Wishes for Baby

Guest Name

Relationship to Parents

Advice for Parents

Wishes for Baby

Guest Name

Relationship to Parents

Advice for Parents

Wishes for Baby

Guest Name

Relationship to Parents

Advice for Parents

Wishes for Baby

Guest Name

Relationship to Parents

Advice for Parents

Wishes for Baby

Guest Name

Relationship to Parents

Advice for Parents

Wishes for Baby

Guest Name

Relationship to Parents

Advice for Parents

Wishes for Baby

Guest Name

Relationship to Parents

Advice for Parents

Wishes for Baby

Guest Name

Relationship to Parents

Advice for Parents

Wishes for Baby

Guest Name

Relationship to Parents

Advice for Parents

Wishes for Baby

Guest Name

____

Relationship to Parents

____

Advice for Parents

____

____

____

Wishes for Baby

____

____

Guest Name

Relationship to Parents

Advice for Parents

Wishes for Baby

Guest Name

Relationship to Parents

Advice for Parents

Wishes for Baby

Guest Name

Relationship to Parents

Advice for Parents

Wishes for Baby

Guest Name

Relationship to Parents

Advice for Parents

Wishes for Baby

Guest Name

Relationship to Parents

Advice for Parents

Wishes for Baby

Guest Name

Relationship to Parents

Advice for Parents

Wishes for Baby

Guest Name

____

Relationship to Parents

____

Advice for Parents

____

____

____

____

Wishes for Baby

____

____

____

Guest Name

Relationship to Parents

Advice for Parents

Wishes for Baby

Notes / Photos

Notes / Photos

Notes / Photos

Notes / Photos

Notes / Photos

Notes / Photos

Notes / Photos

Notes / Photos

Gift Log

Name/Email/Phone   Gift

Gift Log

Name/Email/Phone   Gift

Gift Log

Name/Email/Phone   Gift

Gift Log

Name/Email/Phone   Gift

Gift Log

Name/Email/Phone   **Gift**

Gift Log

Name/Email/Phone   Gift

Gift Log

Name/Email/Phone   Gift

Gift Log

Name/Email/Phone   Gift

Gift Log

Name/Email/Phone   Gift

Gift Log

Name/Email/Phone   Gift